Endorsements

Apostle Marcia Rhoe focuses biographically and yet has portrayed how God's plan is revealed. With seemingly unrelated events, she effectively intensifies our provisionally challenged pathways. She writes of life in which God carefully orchestrates multiple impacts with stress-shifting, phase-oriented challenges which produced a preserved sound, a Godly mind stable in all its ways.

This book, *The Metamorphosis of Purpose* presents developmental information as a conduit of transitional power and strength for change. Without being fear-dominated but truly knowing God's will which brings fully to completion all that He has ordained in you. In reading this book, I hope you come to know God's plan and purpose for your life and to do your assignment.

Bishop Abraham and Priscilla Thomas
No Longer Forsaken Ministries
Charlotte Hall, Maryland

In her book, *The Metamorphosis of Purpose*, Apostle Marcia Rhoe shares some of her life's stories with us, presenting a visual of life in her earliest years and how it profoundly impacted the person she is today. As the author shares the hills and valleys of life, her integrity and honesty paint a clear picture of the transforming grace of God.

Oftentimes, humans only desire to recount the best parts of their story. However, Marcia pulls the curtain back to reveal every phase of development and graciously allows us to view *The Metamorphosis of Purpose*. In the tenderness and transparency of her life's stories, we come away with a realization that we serve a good, good God. Equally, we clearly see that God has a plan for each of our lives, and that plan is working perfectly as we yield to Him.

I encourage you to read this book with an open heart and open mind. You may see portions of your own story in Marcia's as she shares about walking to God, walking with God, and then walking throughout life as God's representative. If we capture that truth, we will comprehend the purpose of life on earth and comprehend Marcia's passion for telling her story of being loved and transformed by Truth.

Dr. Stephen C. Everett
Kingdom Power and Wisdom Center, Cape Coral FL
Apostle, Author, Host of *God's Kingdom* weekly television broadcast.

The Metamorphosis of Purpose

POWER HOUSE

The Metamorphosis of Purpose

DR. MARCIA E. RHOE

Original Cover & Interior Art by Sarah Fernandez for POWER HOUSE, © 2022 Power House Studios, LLC.

Published by:

POWER HOUSE
An imprint of Power House Studios LLC.
thepowerhousestudio.com
PO Box 101678
Cape Coral FL 33910

Home of the Power House Blueprint™–The 90-Days Vision into Sight Concierge Publishing System

Dedication

This book is dedicated to those who were a part of my personal journey but have departed from this life: Gregory J. Edwards, my son whom I loved with all my heart, "G-Money"; Lynwood J. Edwards, Sr., my dad, who gave me the nickname "Brain"; Lynwood J. Edwards, III, my nephew; Ronnie Hall, my nephew; Terrence Plymouth, my grandson, who taught me how to love unconditionally, "TP"; and to all of my family that have departed from this life, the Edwardses, Williamses, and Moores who taught me how to do "Family Business."

Acknowledgments

My husband, Frederick Rhoe, for 48 years of loving me through the process.

My mom, Grace M Edwards, has seen me through all stages of my journey, my sister, Belinda Edwards, and my brother, Lynwood J. Edwards Jr. (Betty).

To my grands Zarycke (Jaydin) Edwards, Tecallian Edwards, and Dextel Gooding; all my nieces and nephews and god-children.

Special Thanks and Appreciation to:

Willie and Doris Jones

Charles and Patricia Durant

Brenda Sutton (my "womb sister")

Shirley Robinson

Clifton Griffin Sr.

Cassandra Rhoe (my "covenant partner")

Aunties: Addie Mae Swinson and Mary Kay Smith

Bishop Elbert and Sandra Kilpatrick

Bishop Leslie and Rebecca Sims

Destiny Ministries Church Family of Kinston, NC

Make-up Artist: Sheri-queenetta Holmes

Attire Coordinator: Belinda Edwards

Photography: Tech Head Photography, LLC

Transcript: Stream Line Media Agency

Publishing and Design: Power House Studios, LLC.

Contents

Introduction

I would look in the mirror, stare, and say, "Who are you?" I would say to my reflection, "Who am I?" For a long time, it seemed that all I heard of was dying and going to my "sweet home in the by and by." They would say, "Give your life to Jesus so you won't go to hell!" I would think, "There has to be more!" Guess what? There is!

In maturing in His Word, I have learned that God's plan is for us to receive, to accept, not only a new beginning but the full and finished work of Jesus! He is the Master-planner, your Creator, the author, and the finisher of our faith. Dare to believe this today!

Peace and well-being are our future and hope. Walking to God, Walking with God, and Walking as God is a three-fold journey that continues throughout a lifetime. In the decades I have lived thus far, God has skillfully, artfully, and compassionately ordered my steps and stages in life. From womb to birth and all the way to where I am now, my steps were predestined and planned in His covenant conversation with Himself. And so were yours!

No matter where you find yourself today, your journey has always been about becoming what God planned. A good life on a good path might not be the path you have traveled thus far. You might have taken some detours. You might feel like you got run off the path by the actions of others. BUT GOD… has a plan for your good!

I am convinced now that every step and everything I go through, He turns it for my good and uses it to lead me to His plan, my purpose, and my Creator. Sometimes we think we control our lives, but the truth is that God orders the footsteps of every child of God. He says to us, "with Love and kindness have I drawn thee" (Jeremiah 31:3).

He desires that we be his ambassadors in the earth. We are here to represent the Father and to do the Father's bidding, to take care of the "family business." We were, you were, chosen before the foundation of the world. It is written, "Now yield and submit to Him" (Job 22:21, AMP). But I like this translation best: "Acquaint now thyself with God" (Job 22:21, ESV).

God wants us to know him more intimately and excellently. He wants to teach us to speak as His representative. What an honor! And, this takes nothing from God; it does not diminish who He is, for, by His Word, heaven and earth must be one. We speak what heaven has released and must bind what heaven has declared unlawful. We must loose what heaven has given the right to come to the earth. Can I say that again? Heaven and earth must be one. While in the earth, we must walk, talk and act as God, fully representing Him and carrying on the Kingdom's Business (Family Business)!

Life is a trust, a test, and a temporary assignment! God is Spirit, but we are created to express Him on the earth. We are the visible of the invisible God. We are his offspring on earth. Walking as God is not arrogance, for as He is, so are we in the earth. I am talking about my position, the position of every born-again believer in Christ Jesus, ruling and reigning in the earth on His behalf! What a glorious reality!

Come with me into His Word and walk through the testimonies of my life where I pray you, too, will discover your own... *Metamorphosis of Purpose!*

Apostle Marcia E. Rhoe

Part One

Walking to God

Chapter One

The Journey Begins

For I know the thoughts that I think toward you,
saith the Lord, thoughts of peace, and not of evil, to
give you an expected end.

(Jeremiah 29:11)

God has a plan for every one of us. His desire to bring
us to His expected end is fulfilled in that plan. Peace and
well-being are our future and hope. I believe my journey in
God's plan started when I left my mother's womb on May 3,
1953. From that time, every person I encountered led me in
some way to my creator, Almighty God Jehovah.

I didn't know that I was walking to God in my early life,
yet by His plan, I was. I can remember living in the country,
and my parents had to work in the field along with my pater-
nal grandparents. They hired others to help harvest the crops.
It did not mean much to me at that time. All I remember was

that no worries or cares entered my mind. I was too young to care about what to eat or wear. My parents made sure that those things were taken care of. I remember starting elementary school at East Green Elementary and being very friendly with my first-grade teacher, whom I looked up to. She had beautiful skin, dressed nice, and wore a lovely, fragrant perfume. It made me feel special.

She saw something in me and made me a part of the musical band for the school, not to play an instrument but to lead the band into the auditorium. That made me feel special. That was my first sign of becoming a leader. I had to dress in a majorette uniform and lead the band. I was very studious; some would call me one of the teacher's favorite students. I didn't know about separation, differences, or distinction. I only did what the teacher asked me to do with my parents' permission. I was being groomed to come to know God. All roads lead to Him.

While living with my father's mother, I could go out to play and explore as far as I could see. They would tell me that "all of this is our inheritance." I could not imagine all this land belonged to us. I would run as far as I could, and I saw the extended family doing what we were doing there. Sometimes, my sister, a cousin, and I would come to a cliff where I could look down and see other families. This is how I knew where our farm stopped. Not only did we have our own family farm, but other families around us had their farms. We were all family.

After seven and a half years, we moved to Kinston, North Carolina. I left the place of wide open lands on the family farm and moved to a city where houses were close together. What a change! Life changed from riding the school bus driven by a family member to walking on cement sidewalks to school. No matter what type of weather, we had to walk to school. Our parents would take us to school if the weather was too bad. We had good hot meals for lunch.

I met new classmates, teachers, and friends. It was not hard for me to adapt to the new environments and people. Looking back, the transition was not complicated. Advancement was not complicated. I was able to advance in this new place.

In my fourth-grade class, we celebrated a festival called "The May Pole Day," where all classes had to do an activity to celebrate that day. My class danced in black leotards and shirts with long black tails dressed as monkeys. We had to dance and keep rhythm. What a task! We had to work in oneness and think as a team. These sweet memories still bring to mind the song "Lollipop" from 1958 and its lyrics, "Lollipop, Lollipop oh Lolli, Lolli, Lolli, Lollipop.[1]"

In fifth grade, I was chosen as the queen of my class. My mother had a beautiful violet-colored dress made. She made sure I was the most beautiful queen of the 5th grade. I was proud to wear that crown to represent my class. Those were great times, learning about life and why I am here. Still,

---

1 Chordettes, "Lollipop," Cadence, 1958

many years later, I continue to learn about my Creator and why I am here.

Walking to God is how I started this, by remembering my beginnings. Moving to Kinston also introduced me to limitations and restrictions that I had not known before. I was learning to trust others and not just my family. My world was expanding. I began seeing the world through the many lenses of others. My growth and development and social skills helped me to walk to God.

While in junior high school, I became a part of the musical band and dance group. I learned to play the clarinet and won dance contests. My world was enlarging with new teachers and new friends. I remember specifically carrying over one of my old friendships to add to my new friendships. I had three good friends and then many more were added to my list. I learned different ideas from them. I looked at boys of my age and knew they were around, but I was not yet interested in them at that season in my life. I was still learning to balance school, chores, and becoming responsible in the family. As the eldest of my siblings, it was my place to set a standard for my sister and brother. What a big job!

As I moved on to senior high school (my ninth through twelfth grade), my interests changed. I found that young guys were checking me out, and I felt appreciated. My eyes opened to the newness—the new seasons of growth, development, and discovery. I discovered that my thoughts and ideas were changing. I was still walking to God. Whether good or bad,

I had to make good choices based on what I saw and learned from my parents and others.

My 9th grade English class had an assignment of learning the poem "The Creation" by James Weldon Johnson (1871–1938). I studied and learned the poem. We had to recite it, and I got an A+. I call this ministering before people. I became one with these people and made it my own with various dramatics. The entire class was impressed with me. Their response was with tears, and I cried while performing. I was connected with my class but I didn't stop there. I kept performing. What was happening? God was opening my eyes. I was coming to realize TRUTH, which later I knew was God.

I moved from the classroom to the church, sharing the poem from church to church. This was new to me, performing before a large group, but I gained a significant following. Some might have called me a developing traveling evangelist.

Can you imagine? I had captivated the audience with my words and actions. I was blessed with the power of influence and persuasion; this was like a revival. I was touched, and now I had sponsors that wanted to reward me for such a moving, heartfelt drama. Still, this was not daunting to me that this was my journey of walking to God and, eventually, walking with God. God knew because He had this plan for my life.

In 10th grade, I met my first love. I ended up getting pregnant. It was a devastating time. The idea of suicide came to my mind. My loving mother stopped me from the act. My friends stood by me through the entire experience. This was my introduction to covenant and caring relationships as I was walking to God.

My parents loved me despite my choices. They showed so much love. When they saw my 5 lb. 15-ounce baby boy was born, they rejoiced. How did I see the world in that moment? I saw forgiveness as if I had done no wrong. My parents even had a "Sweet 16" birthday party for me. I received so many gifts. So many people came out to support me; that love and support brought healing to me. That love kept me as I was walking to God.

What did I see? This was like the parable of the prodigal sons in Luke 15:11–32. I was restored to a place and a position with no shame or blame. I received forgiveness, and I felt whole. I graduated from high school with my class in 1971. I never missed a grade or repeated a grade.

I was still walking to God. The Lord had His hands on me from birth until now. As high school was completed, I now see that **I was walking into my purpose, destiny, and unto my creator. The purpose of God still goes on.**

Chapter Two

Every Step Leads To Him

For He will complete what He appoints for me,
and many such things are in His mind.

(Job 23:14, ESV)

Every step we take leads us to God, who is our creator. We might not know that in our beginnings. But I am convinced now that every step and everything I go through leads to God's plan. Sometimes we think we control our lives, but the truth is that God orders the footsteps of every child of God. God says to us, "therefore with Lovingkindness have I drawn thee" (Jeremiah 31:3). Our steps are truly ordered by the Lord, but He knows the way that we must take. (That is in Job 23:10.) We go forward based on the teaching through the years.

After graduating from high school, I went to Washington, D.C., to live with my extended family for a while. My parents wanted me home, and my child needed me, so I moved back to Kinston. I was 19 years old, staying with my parents, with no job and a child who needed me. I knew I had to make some decisions.

Right about then, my mother suggested we attend a two-week revival. Can you imagine? A two-week revival with services every night! I went to appease my mother the first week, but the second week was different. That week, my answer to God was "YES!" I felt a tug on my heart on March 10, 1972. That day, my whole world changed. This was the day I responded to God's leading for my life.

Apostle Bobby Kittrell of LaGrange, NC, was the guest speaker. He preached from Hebrews 2:3, asking us, "How shall we escape if we neglect so great salvation; which at first began to be spoken by the Lord, and was confirmed unto us by them that heard him?"

The other saints were so happy to have a teen respond to the power of God. I was the first young lady of my age in this Pentecostal church. Before then, the church primarily consisted of married couples, older widows, and older single women. But they welcomed me. I was led to Christ by the Mothers in the church. I didn't know anything concerning what God wanted for me, but I gave myself totally to the church and the things of the Lord.

Looking back, they were legalistic concerning dress code and faithfulness to the local church. But this had positive benefits in my life at the time. They expected me to be an example, a model, and an inspiration to others. I understood my responsibility was to all, including the entire church family. I began to seek God and pattern after the older saints in the church.

In that Pentecostal setting, it was normal to preach against outward adorning. Seeing the older believers' dress code was an example for all believers in that setting. The older saints established their doctrine mainly from the Old Testament, but at the heart of the doctrine was the truth that it was important to them to make a difference between the world and the church. When I say the world, I'm speaking about how life was before being born again. They strongly emphasized the scripture in 2 Corinthians 6:17, "'Wherefore come out from among them and be ye separate,' saith the Lord, 'touch not the unclean thing; and I will receive you.'"

So, to their understanding, the unclean things were makeup, jewelry, and other things. Taken from the Old Testament, in Exodus 32:1–4, makeup and jewelry related to the idols that the children of Israel made in the wilderness. With that understanding, makeup identified with the pagan lifestyle. Separating from this was an outward sign that you identified with a changed life. Looking back, some of this had merit for that time. It established priorities in my life and taught me about being set apart by God.

I got a job, but at the time, since I could not wear jewelry, makeup, or up-to-date clothes, I wanted very few material things. So, instead, I spent most of my wages helping my parents. It was my choice; I wanted to be a help. I wanted to be a leader among my siblings and take responsibility. I learned to be dependable, consistent, and faithful. I practiced these traits with God, my family, and the community.

The community was another place I began to grow and become an influence with the love of God. While growing up, after believing and praying for a relationship with my child's father, I had to come to terms with the truth—this was not God's plan. So, I put that to rest and I moved forward. I started working with the youth in the community. During a summer week, the neighborhood children came faithfully and were rewarded for their attendance. We sang, danced, and had a good time with the Lord. It was a fun time with cookouts and gatherings. The children enjoyed that, and these outreaches made a difference in the community.

We saw that it was not just reaching the children. The children were coming to church and bringing their parents. The church began to grow. Going to prayer meetings and Bible studies, I was the only single young lady in the church until one day, I was asked to read the scripture and pray during the Bible study services. I did not know or understand how to pray. I began to mimic the older ones. These Thursday night gatherings were growing, and more people were attending. The services were growing rapidly, and I was growing rapidly. My understanding began to increase.

In Matthew 7:7–8 (ESV), I learned that we could "ask, and it will be given to you; seek, and you will find; knock, and it will be opened to you. For everyone who asks, receives, and the one who seeks finds, and to the one who knocks, it will be opened."

The logos—the written Word of God—was coming to life. The Logos was becoming my Rhema. Logos in Greek is often translated into English as logic or an inspired written word. Still, it can also mean a thought, reason, principle, or standard. So, really the entire Bible is Logos. You can read the written word and get information, principles, and standards, but the Rhema Word takes you deeper than what is written!

Rhema (also from Greek) is the spoken utterance unveiling the written word. Romans 10:17 says, "So then faith cometh by hearing, and hearing by the Word (Rhema) of God." And Hebrews 4:12 says, "For the word of God is quick, and powerful, and sharper than any two-edged sword, piercing even to the dividing asunder of the soul and spirit, and of the joints and marrow, and is a discerner of the thoughts and intents of the heart."

Psalms 119:103 says, "The entrance of thy word giveth light. It gives understanding unto the simple." I also like the New International Version of this same verse: "The unfolding of your words gives light." This is the Rhema. It gives understanding to the simple.

Jesus is the living logos. John 1:1 says, "In the beginning was the Word, and the word was with God, and the Word was God." Psalm 40:7 and Hebrews 10:7 say, "Then said I,

Lo, I come (in the volume of the book, it is written of me) to do thy will, O God."

When unveiling God's word, it gives revelation of the written Word as John says in Revelation 1:3, "Blessed is he that readeth, and they that hear the word of this prophecy and keep those things which are written therein: For the time is at hand." The first verse of the book of Revelation states that it's "The revelation of Jesus Christ." The Rhema in the Revelation is to get a crystal-clear understanding of Jesus Christ.

I began to teach the things I understood. The pastor saw how The Word was using me and asked me to teach Bible study. So, we would pray and study the Bible. The unsaved and young people began coming to the services. Husbands were now coming with their wives and children. God ordered our steps. I still did not know exactly what I was doing or what was going on with me, but I knew it was a change—a good change! Even though I looked like Marcia and walked like Marcia, I knew I was different; I was being changed!

When I read the Word, something would happen to me inwardly. I started to see it in a different light. I was learning more and more. I attended other churches and developed a greater hunger. My ordered steps made a difference. I sought God even more and could not get enough. I learned about fasting, prayer meetings, and more about the ways of God.

I started communicating with God to give me the wisdom to help my family, church family, and community. I was so caught up in this that my mind was equally caught up in looking for Jesus. I was sold out!

I wanted my family to know this Jesus I was beginning to know! **I wanted this for my family, and I still today desire this for you all... to experience the fullness of Jesus as the unfolding of His Word gives you Light.**

Chapter Three

How Do I See the World?

And we know that all things work together for good
to them that love God, to them who are the called
according to his purpose.

(Romans 8:28)

My life has had many turns, but I believe God causes all things to work together for my good. My early world consisted of first knowing God, loving my parents, and seeing life through their eyes. My father was a very compassionate and loving man. He showed love to his children. He worked hard to see that we had everything we needed and extra. My father looked out for his family.

Remember, he came from a family that owned property. He had sisters that attended college and owned many worldly effects. They were self-sufficient. His siblings looked out for

15

him, ensuring he had all he needed and wanted. When my father was born, his oldest sister was 20 years old. He grew up with his nieces and nephews. Some would suggest my dad was spoiled or greatly loved and privileged. So, he repeated the same with his children, but I did not recognize this growing up. As his children, we saw life as normal, with no difference. I am sure we had difficult times growing up, but I did not see it. These are spiritual principles. That's how my heavenly Father sees us. He loves us, protects us, and guides us; He highly favors us.

Things changed when we moved to Kinston with no close friends. My father became close to the neighbors. From his working experience on the farm, he learned to operate tractors. He learned to be a carpenter and a plumber. He was a diligent man and had his own business. How I see the world was formed by what God showed me through the lives of those around me. I saw hard work, consistency, and accountability. My father left his inheritance and separated from his family to have his legacy.

There is entrepreneurship in my DNA, thanks to my uncle and father. My two aunts graduated from high school as valedictorians. One of my aunts wrote drama plays and directed them. I see myself as someone with that type of tenacity, and all these influences shaped how I see the world.

I am not sure who started the tradition, but when I was born, my Aunt Minnie took me in her arms with items in hand. Everyone born in the family received the same tradition, which continues today. Still talking about how I see the world, we as a family had this belief and tradition that every child born in the family would be dedicated to God by a family member. They would take a child of only a few months old with a pencil in the right hand, a dollar in the left hand, and the Bible under the child's head. They walked around the house and spoke prophetically with the words of blessing, prosperity, and the future for that child.

I saw the same thing in the mini-series, ROOTS. Kunta Kinte is a character in the 1976 novel, "Roots: The Saga of an American Family," by American author Alex Haley. Kunta Kinte (portrayed by actor LeVar Burton) did the same dedication for his first child, Kizzy. Holding her up before God, he spoke words about her life's journey. I see that the same tradition and understanding of this powerful act can be more than just a tradition but ministry. So, an individual must be a God-fearing person knowing the ways of God and understanding purpose and destiny. This cannot be just a religious act, but it is ministry when the truth is revealed.

I see the principle in my own family as in Genesis 27:27–29, where Isaac blessed his son. It is not done much now like earlier in my life, but I see the principle of blessing loved ones. Whenever I stand before God's people, I bless them with God's word, speaking about their inheritance and benefits in Christ Jesus.

My mother's parents had their land and property and were hard workers. They saved year after year to build a house in Kinston. It's the same house from when I was seven years old. I still remember it vividly. It was a six-room house with one bath. What a great accomplishment! So, being responsible, consistent, and having endurance and accountability is how I saw my world.

My grandmother Mary was raised by her eldest sister and uncle. Their life was full of insecurity and fear without their parents' love. So, they learned to trust in the Lord for everything. I learned to pray and seek God from her. How do I see my world? In Grandmother Mary, I saw much hard work, faithfulness, and diligence. She was a big tither. Grandma Mary believed in tithing faithfully. When she learned the principle of sowing and reaping, she remained faithful until her transition. I'm faithful, just like my grandmother!

My Grandma Elena was a follower of God, and while I never heard of her giving tithes, she was a churchgoer. Grandma Mary would tithe everything, and Grandma Elena not so much. How do I see my world? We honor the Lord by giving first. I learned this from Grandma Mary, who was faithful to her church. I also learned consistency in faith from Grandma Mary—she was strict in her faith.

Both grandmothers had a relationship with God, but it looked different. One grandmother was religiously strict. She kept all the church doctrines and traditions of that organization. She expected to keep the Ten Commandments to the letter. I guess that was how she understood living the Christian life. At the same time, the other grandmother was liberal and showed much more compassion. Initially, I carried both characteristics as I began walking with God. I have a new perspective now. **God changes our perspective as we walk with Him.**

Chapter Four

Broken but Healed

Come, and let us return unto the Lord: for He hath
torn, and He will heal us; He hath smitten, and He
will bind us up.

(Hosea 6:1)

At the age of sixteen, the mothers in the church asked me
to stand in front of the congregation and apologize for my
actions that led to the birth of my son—and I did. At first, I
was nervous, ashamed, and embarrassed. A lot of other emotions were going on as well. My first thoughts were, "What
will the family think about me? How much shame and dis-
grace did it bring to the family?"

I always wanted to be approved and accepted by them. I
heard about other young girls that got pregnant. They were
rejected, abandoned, and cast aside by their families, even out

of sight when people visited. They could not be seen or heard until visitors were gone. Being pregnant was not enough; being rejected was worse. Can you imagine the number of times suicidal thoughts came to me? I thank God that did not happen. Many family members were in that church because it was a family church. I found that I was accepted, not rejected.

Not long after my son was born, I was asked to go before the church for forgiveness and to be restored. You may say, "Why the church?" Even though I was not yet a confessed believer, I sang in the youth choir, ushered in the church, and do not forget that at the age of fourteen, I did a one-person drama of the poem, "The Creation." Yes, I was very active in the church. The leaders had great expectations of me. I looked to leadership as God's representatives, so it was in my heart to comply with the request.

Obedience to authority and honor to the elders and mothers of the fellowship took me a long way. Through obedience, I could feel the warmth of love and healing. Many saw it as embarrassment, but I saw it as making things right. Many could not see doing that, and they didn't. But I looked at this moment as healing, cleansing, and freedom. That is what I experienced as an act of obedience.

Looking back, God prepared me for even greater and better things. My view of life was changing. In Ephesians 5:26, Paul spoke of the cleansing of the church with the washing of the water of the Word. Even though Paul was talking about one point, I believe it was equally about cleansing, healing, and freedom—it was about making things right. I believe that there was no limit to the cleansing because of the events that took place. I was broken for righteousness. It purified me and took away all shame and blame.

The process changed me from the inside out. Because of my willingness to obey, these scriptures became real to me.

When God speaks of obedience, it is His command. "Samuel replied: 'Does the Lord delight in burnt offerings and sacrifices as much as in obeying the Lord? To obey is better than sacrifice and to heed is better than the fat of rams'" (1 Samuel 15:22).

Hebrews 13:17 says, "Obey them that have the rule over you, and submit yourselves: for they watch for your souls, as they that must give account, that they may do it with joy, and not with grief: for that is unprofitable for you."

How did I see myself? I opened completely to the mothers! Nothing would stop me from this small task. I had no shame and no worry about what the others would say. I just had to obey leadership. Looking back, I obeyed those that had the rule over me. I saw it like this: Those people may be the ones to lead you to greatness.

This is how I saw myself. God ordered my steps. Psalms 37:23–24 says, "The steps of a good man are ordered by the Lord: and he delighteth in his way. Though he fall, he shall not be utterly cast down: for the Lord upholdeth him with his hand." God always brought me to Himself; even when I didn't know it, He was shaping my destiny. We are supposed to do so much more than we are doing. As of now, we are just in seed form. We must trust His timing to reveal what He has for us. If the seed is watered, it will grow. The seed will grow and blossom. With the right support system, it will get all it needs.

God has planned all this. Have you ever seen the play or the film, The Wizard of Oz? In a sense, as a metaphor, we must do as Dorothy did and "follow the yellow brick road[2]," which in real life, means to follow God's plan for your life. Following His plan and watering the seed will help you come forth and be who God called you to be. You will succeed. It was destined and predetermined. Romans 8:29 says, "For whom He did foreknow, He also did predestinate to be conformed to the image of His Son, that he might be the first-born among many brethren."

We are in the image of His Son. We were broken, separated, and now, we are healed. Jeremiah 30:17 says, "'For I will restore health unto thee, and I will heal thee of thy wounds,' saith the Lord; 'because they called thee an Outcast,' saying, 'This is Zion, whom no man seeketh after.'"

Hosea 6:1–2 says, "Come, and let us return unto the Lord: for He hath torn, and He will heal us; He hath smitten, and He will bind us up. After two days will He revive us: In the third day He will raise us up, and we shall live in His sight."

---

2   Harold Arlen, E.Y. Harburg, "We're Off to See the Wizard" (1939)

What am I saying? How do I see myself now? **We are covenant people. Trust the process.**

Part Two

Walking with God

Chapter Five

The Big Question

Beloved, now are we the sons of God, and it doth
not yet appear what we shall be: but we know that,
when He shall appear, we shall be like Him; for we
shall see Him as He is.

(1 John 3:2)

Sometimes I would look in the mirror, standing there
staring; I would say, "Who are you?" And then I would ask,
"Who am I?"

There is only one thread that connects us to our destiny.
That thread is God. When you seek Him and desire to do His
will, all paths lead to Him. Knowing this removes all stress,
frustration, doubt, and wondering about your life. Many
questions are answered when you know who is in charge.
Life would have been easier if I had been told that years ago.
It is impossible to figure out who you are without knowing

HIM (Christ). God is the planner and author of each life. We must trust the process.

Life is a trust, a test, and a temporary assignment. Learning to trust God is difficult for some. But for others, it isn't that complicated. Philippians 1:6 says, "Being confident of this very thing, that He which hath begun a good work in you will perform it until the day of Jesus Christ." This speaks of His confidence to finish what He started. Confidence has full trust in the one that is in charge. Since God is in charge, we can have full confidence in Him.

As I walked with God, I met a certain young man, Frederick Rhoe. We discovered that we both loved God and that we each longed to grow in our spiritual appetites more and more. Can you imagine? Walking with someone with the same thoughts, beliefs, and trust in the God whom you are walking with? We have been married now for many decades, but our shared uncommon hunger for God brought us together and across the path of the late Bishop Paul Gaskins.

In 1975, we met Bishop Gaskins from Washington DC. He was a very inspiring man of God. He was so full of love and compassion for us. Bishop Gaskins was gifted in the Word of God. He introduced us to the teachings on covenantal relationships in the Kingdom of God. He was infectious and like a magnet. People were drawn to him and spent time with him. We found that people were drawn to us as well. This man of God was so full of life. Because of our relationship, it expanded to another level in worship.

We learned different songs. We had great freedom in worship and praise. As we walked with Bishop Gaskins, there was a song for every situation. Our minds were opened, and we started writing songs like: "On a clear day you can see the move of the Lord," written and copyrighted by Frederick Rhoe. It was a new day, and we could see life more clearly. Bishop Gaskins wrote and introduced his songs, one in particular, "This Is The Day, This Glorious Day." We learned many songs and wrote many songs. Our songs were about what we enjoyed and experienced in the Lord. What a great time we had.

He also brought much structure to us as a newly married couple. We learned how to communicate with each other concerning marital issues. Remember, we were a young couple, only married for two years. The church did not deal with certain challenges in the family setting that young couples dealt with. However, Bishop Gaskins was there walking with us through so much. I believe we are married today because of his ministry. (We celebrate forty-eight years of marriage as I write this book). Thank you, Jesus!

We learned to help many couples navigate through their relationships from this relationship. We learned how to guard, guide, and govern in relationships, not only in knowledge but in our example to others. Because of his teachings, we have incorporated marriage counseling, single retreats, and youth ministries into our ministry. If there is one word to describe Bishop Paul Gaskins, it is "relationships." He was a man of fellowship. He showed us that God is not about religion (having a form of religion) but relationships. God wants a family of many sons and daughters.

When we met Bishop Gaskins, we attended separate churches but desired to be in one fellowship. We spoke with our pastors and asked to be released so that we could be a part of one ministry. Both pastors agreed to release us, and the relationship continued.

One must understand the context of these decisions. I would not decide without consulting with leadership because of my upbringing. Even back when my husband and I first started dating, there was no consideration about marriage until we went before the elders. Not only did we seek approval from the elders but also from friends that knew us. As we walked with God, our mindsets were submitted to spiritual government and accountability.

We learned that we were free to wear makeup and play basketball without sinning. We heard teachings on covenant. We began fellowshipping with believers on the weekend, enjoying cookouts, and going to the beach with swim-wear! Oh, what joy we were experiencing! We could laugh, have fun, and remain saved. Later, the covenant teachings we heard placed us in a unique situation. We, as a couple, entered a covenantal relationship with another couple. Three things happened to us, or should I say, took place in us. We learned more about separation, endurance, and accountability. (I address these three words more a bit later, in Chapter 8.)

We were learning and experiencing so many new things. As we learned new songs, we lifted our hands while singing. We cried in worship services. And we didn't fight the devil day and night anymore. Oh, what a change! I knew about prayer, but praise enhanced our devotion and private time with the Lord. We were becoming FREE and even freer! We weren't fulfilling our desires but the Lord's desire.

We were learning that we were created to worship Him. With praise, our hearts were opened more and more to Abba Father. As we opened ourselves to Him, He filled that space with Himself. Finding out we were sons of God just blew my mind! I knew that Jesus was His Son. But now, we learn we are the Father's sons through the death, burial, and resurrection of Jesus Christ! Oh, my goodness, this was too much for us to handle, but the loving presence of God in the midst helped us learn Christ Jesus, Our Lord. This was rich.

You see, other ministers from our past background did not tell us these things, but God had His appointed time. I can truly say from Galatians 1:15–16, "But when it pleased God who separated me from my mother's womb to reveal his Son in me that I may preach him among the heathen."

We learned that "Moses gave the law, but grace and truth came by Jesus Christ" (John 1:17). Listen to this same verse from the Amplified Bible, "For the law was given through Moses, but the grace (the unearned, undeserved, favor of God) and truth came through Jesus Christ."

And then, I heard, "You don't have to work for your freedom, healing, and wholeness. It was given as a gift from Jesus Christ to deliver and set you free!" Working for it would have meant I earned something. But it is free, so I didn't have to wear myself out. Oh, what a release it was to hear that! I was walking with God in the Rhema Word of Ephesians 2:8–9, "For by grace are ye saved that not of yourself not of works lest any man should boast."

It's not who I was, but who Jesus is that did all this for me! **This revelation separates us from manufactured, artificial doctrines into a more perfect understanding of grace.**

Chapter Six

Knowing Him

Seek ye the Lord while He may be found. Call ye
upon him while He is near.

(Isaiah 55:6)

Walking with God has been an awesome experience. I
used to think God was far off, untouchable, and unapproach-
able. Even the children of Israel felt the same way while in
the wilderness. For example, they believed death came if one
attempted to touch Him or look upon His face. He was the
God of the mountains and the valleys. Israel knew Him that
way but struggled to see Him as a father. The name Father
is a name of endearment. When I think of a father, I see my
father as a provider, a protector, loving, guiding, and very
close to me with compassion. Now I know that's my heavenly
Father's character.

My earthly father loved his family and would do anything to provide for them. My thoughts about my dad were of warm feelings and safety. If we were disciplined, he would hug us and love us. He said, "Daddy loves you, and Daddy wants you to do your best and be your best." He didn't chastise us much, but his loving, stable, and consistent voice kept us in order. He did not raise his hand much, but it was with a loving embrace with the necessary discipline when he did. We knew how much Dad loved us by the way he hugged us. He was the youngest of ten children, and all his siblings protected and loved him, which he, in turn, gave his children.

My mom was more of a disciplinarian. It was just the opposite with my father. My dad would go a while before disciplining us. He just didn't want to do that. He desired to draw us closer. This reminded me of the scripture in Jeremiah 31:3: "Yea have I loved thee, with an everlasting love: therefore with loving kindness have I drawn thee." I respected the man he was.

Seeing how my dad loved us made it easy to understand my heavenly Father's love. After coming to know Him, I walked with Him. The love of God was not hard to embrace. I sometimes think how you see your earthly father greatly influences how you see your heavenly Father. If you see your parents as strict, stiff, hard, and not much compassion, it can cause you at times and moments not to open your heart to your heavenly Father. We forget that the God of love gave everything to demonstrate His love for us. "For God so loved the world that he gave his only begotten Son" (John 3:16).

As I have stated, my first view of fatherhood was my natural father. My father demonstrated provision, protection, guidance, and government. Your parents are your first authority figures and examples in life. You glean from their lives. My natural father knew me at birth, but my heavenly Father knew me before birth. Jeremiah 1:5 says, "Before I formed thee in the belly I knew thee; and before thou camest forth out of the womb I sanctified thee, and I ordained thee a prophet unto the nations." My earthly father gave out of his little substance, but my Heavenly Father gave of His unlimited grace, which is far greater.

I saw my dad as a giver. He didn't hold back anything. He gave his best and always loved to that same level. In Acts 20:35, The Word says, "I have shewed you all things, how that so labouring ye ought to support the weak, and to remember the words of the Lord Jesus, how he said, it is more blessed to give than to receive." I saw that in my earthly father's ways. Dad took us out to talk, laugh, and play games. He would have fun with us. But remember, Dad came from a family that was not strict with rules and regulations. They would not dot every "i" and cross every "t." If you were wrong, they took the time to teach you before you had hard discipline.

In contrast, my mom grew up in a family that ensured that the family would dot every "i" and cross every "t." So, I am a combination of both families. As I walk with God,

I see both sides working in me. As I continue, I see how much God loves me. His love outweighs the strong, hard discipline and covers a multitude of sins. Sometimes I was very much loved, but I was always mindful to stick with the Law (what we know as the 10 Commandments). I believed that if I performed the Law, I would be in good graces and in right standing with God. The law sometimes overrode my love for people; however, I would return to compassion for them. I found I would be tossed back and forth. I switched from grace to law or from law to grace. Do you know that will wear you out?

But then I heard someone say, "the law was given by Moses, but grace and truth came by Jesus Christ" (John 1:17). That hit me like a ton of bricks. I stopped and said, "What?!"

It was different! There was no more of the roller coaster life going up and down or riding the merry-go-round. It was different—just different. Moses gave the Law, but Jesus brought grace and truth. Grace is unmerited and unearned favor—debt-free. What a revelation! I was shocked to learn that God the Father gave His Son to set me free! He gave me stability and forgiveness. Jesus completely set me free. I did not have to work on anything to obtain this liberty. My, my! The laboring was over. Trying to do it myself had come to an end. Thank you, Jesus!

After the Father gave His Son to set me free, Jesus the Son gave his life for me. Jesus is the Giver. Then, I found other benefits: forgiveness that paid for my sins in full. He not only saved me but healed and delivered me. WOW! Knowing that someone took my place and gave me their place was a lot for me. He was my scapegoat and sacrificial offering. I no longer had to struggle to ensure I did everything right. Jesus made it right by his obedience to our heavenly Father.

Now the scriptures, God's Holy Word, became real to me. I wanted to know more. My hunger for His Word caused me to spend more and more time with Him. This is called: walking with God. This hunger brought me into the presence of great teachers of the Word.

I started reading different translations of the Bible. I read the Amplified, the New International Version, and the Message. They all made the message clearer and easier to understand. God was enlarging my capacity for Him and filling it with Himself.

My, my, my! Not only was I growing and being fed, but my husband was too. We used to say, "Is this real or what?" I was not just learning in Sunday School and early prayer. We were hooked for more and more of Jesus. And God delivered!

I distinctly remember one week in September 1978. We were painting our new home. We were also listening to the gospel hour on the radio. The next voice that came on was teaching about the seven separations of Abraham. I had never heard anything like that before. We ordered the series and later met Pastor Kelley Varner from Richlands, North Carolina. He lived about twenty miles from us. We got a chance to check out the man of God. Before we entered the sanctuary, he came and said, "You must be Brother Rhoe, and this is your wife?" Oh My God! What? He had never seen us before that moment. He must have known us by the Spirit of God. He asked us to join him for service.

We walked in at the time of worship, and everybody was standing with raised hands, dancing, and worshiping the Lord. Their approach to worship was new to us. During the service, the pastor called Fred, my husband, forward and began to prophesy to him. Then he called me up and told me to sing the song of the Lord. So, I guess I looked like I could sing. I had never heard the song of the Lord. I had heard the prophetic in times past. Preachers would prophesy about houses, cars, and financial blessings. This was different.

When the pastor asked me to sing, I believed just him saying, "Sing," caused the Spirit of God to come upon me. God touched my tongue, and my mouth flowed like a river. This was new to me. We were so blessed and shared all that happened with our pastor and church family. The next month the entire church went to see this pastor. A fellowship and relationship were formed from this gathering. We all would go to this church and be blessed from time to time. That church opened to the surrounding churches and fellowships during their School of Ministry. We were meeting and hearing all these ministries from everywhere, expounding on the Word of God. We started reading the Old Testament, which we previously would not read unless it were Psalms or

Proverbs. Maybe, sometimes we would read Genesis, but to read and understand the Old Testament, we never did that. We were fascinated by Abraham, Samuel, Joshua, and other Old Testament patriarchs as we studied God's Word afresh.

Learning about Abraham and Sarah and their journey was especially interesting. They were separated from their family as directed by God. Both of their names were changed, and they were blessed. Abraham heard a voice that he had never heard before. It caused him to make this transition. Like many of my own life's testimonies that you will read in this book, Abraham and Sarah were experiencing walking to God and walking with God. Abraham was not yet walking as God's representative, but can you see the significance of Abraham and everyone else following the same pattern? I believe that this is the order of humanity.

Matthew 11:28–30 says, "Come unto me, all ye that labour and are heavy laden, and I will give you rest. Take my yoke upon you, and learn of me; for I am meek and lowly in heart: and ye shall find rest unto your souls. For my yoke is easy, and my burden is light."

In a new light of understanding, we heard the word rest. This word rest was added to the many other things we were learning. We were to rest in Him and learn of Him. He was the King in His Kingdom. We learned how Jesus operated in God's Kingdom. We saw Him operate with authority by healing the sick and the oppressed. Jesus spoke to multitudes and showed the Love of God. He had compassion for the lost, the forsaken, and the ostracized. Jesus brought big changes to the people who followed him by showing his Heavenly Father's love to them. We experience the same thing by walking with God. We came to know more about our Heavenly Father's love by learning about Jesus. John 15:13 says, "Greater love hath no man than this, that a man lay down his life for his friends." Jesus demonstrated the greater love as he laid down his life so we could have life.

The benefits of walking with God are so amazing. Look at the things we received! We received an identity, security, purpose, acceptance, encouragement, provision, rest, etc. Guess what? It is all in the house (family of God), or I should say, "It is in us in seed form."

Jesus came to release the benefits inside us and through us. As sons of God, we express the invisible by bringing it to visibility. People see what is not seen through us. Romans 1:20 says, "For the invisible things of him from the creation of the world are clearly seen, being understood by the things that are made, even His eternal power and Godhead; so that they are without excuse:"

The greatest and highest position we have in the Kingdom of God is being a son. Jesus made this available for us to experience. One of the Greek names for sons is *Huios*. He's a fully mature son that can carry on the family business and represent the Heavenly Father and His kingdom.

After knowing God, you come to know who you are. This knowledge comes from being in Christ Jesus. **You are so much more than what you thought!**

Chapter Seven

Becoming Partners

And if children, then heirs; heirs of God, and joint-
heirs with Christ; if so be that we suffer with him,
that we may be also glorified together.

(Romans 8:17)

What is an heir? An heir is a person who is legally enti-
tled to goods, properties, and/or rank of another upon that
person's death. The heir(s) inherit and continue the legacy of
the Predecessor.

Who is an heir? Children, descendants, or other close rel-
atives of the deceased are usually heirs. This truth is revealed
in Galatians 4:7, which reads, "Wherefore thou art no more a
servant, but a son; and if a son, then an heir of God through
Christ."

Christ is the avenue that brings us to God. "For Christ
also hath once suffered for sins, the just for the unjust, that

he might bring us to God, being put to death in the flesh, but quickened by the Spirit" (1 Peter 3:18). Because we have returned to God, we are sons and not servants. So, we, as sons of God, are His heirs. Jesus Christ shares His inheritance with us, making us co-heirs with him. In the Old Testament, the heirs were biological sons. The firstborn typically bore the birthright, which meant he was heir to a double portion. We must understand that the true reality of the double portion teaching centers around the concept of the firstborn. Israel was called God's firstborn son in the Old Testament.

Jesus is the firstborn in the New Testament. Because we are co-heirs with Christ, we are a church of firstborn ones. Ephesians 1:11 tells us that our birthright is to have God's inheritance. Yes, we all share the birthright as a firstborn. The birthright's promise to God's people is an image, dominion, and participation in God's kingdom.

In Deuteronomy 21:15–17, the firstborn would receive the inheritance even when the firstborn was born through a hated wife. He must receive the right of the firstborn. This was the law when the children were preparing to enter the Promised Land. But before the Mosaic Law, in Genesis 21:10, Sarah told Abraham, "Cast out this slave woman with her son, for the son of this slave woman shall not be heir with my son, Isaac." The son of the slave woman was Ishmael. He was fourteen years older than Isaac, which was Sarah's firstborn. Isaac wasn't Abraham's firstborn, which created an issue. However, the heir had to be the firstborn to a legitimate wife and not a concubine. Sarah was the legitimate wife. She could make this demand of her husband.

Now, as we look at this, Jesus had to be the firstborn of the legitimate parents for him to be heir to the inheritance of the Father. God sent His only begotten Son to die to bring God and the family (legitimate family) together. When the Father says, "My only begotten Son," He talks about Jesus from John 3:16. The word "MY" shows the connection between Jesus and his Father. Jesus was the Word that became flesh. This was the Father's glory—Jesus was full of His Father's grace and glory. Moses was Elohim's servant, but Jesus was Elohim's Son! "ONLY" means no other begotten son but Jesus. Before Jesus, all men of greatness that God used were servants. Only Jesus met the requirements to be called a mature Son. However, Adam was called the son of God in Luke 3:38. He didn't stay in fellowship with God and became a prodigal. After Genesis 3, Adam became a waster because of his disobedience.

Let's consider the word begotten as it is used regarding the birth of Jesus. "BEGOTTEN" means uniquely born or one of a kind. Jesus was not born of natural birth or naturally involving human conception with a man and a woman. Check this out. John 1:13–14 says, "Which were born, not of blood, nor of the will of the flesh, nor of the will of man, but of God. And the Word was made flesh, and dwelt among us, (and we beheld his glory, the glory as of the only begotten of the Father,) full of grace and truth." Luke 1:34–35 says,

"Then said Mary unto the angel, 'How shall this be, seeing I know not a man?' And the angel answered and said unto her, 'The Holy Ghost shall come upon thee, and the power of the Highest shall overshadow thee: therefore also that holy thing which shall be born of thee shall be called the Son of God.'"

I am saying all that to show that Jesus is the link to the Father. John 14:6 says, "Jesus saith unto him, 'I am the way, the truth, and the life: no man cometh unto the Father, but by me.'" Without him, there would be no joining or a link to the Father (ABBA). Jesus's obedience to the Father's will opened a new door to bring a family to God. God had servants, but now He has His first Son, bringing other sons to Him. Jesus did not come by the will of the flesh but by the Father's will. When I made the connection, it just blew my religious mind!

The family expects the older child to be an example for the younger siblings in the natural world. In some cases, that was not so. My parents taught me to be a leader for my younger sister and brother. I spent a lot of time with my dad. I guess I was Daddy's girl. He would call me "Brain," which became my nickname. That did not make me better, but the weight of that positioned me for leadership. By nature, there was a determination in me to excel.

In high school, one of my friend's fathers worked at DuPont. I saw all the nice clothes she wore. She looked like she had it all. I remember saying, "When I grow up, I will get a job at DuPont." So, I did. In another instance, my mother trusted me to go to the Post Office and buy stamps. After walking into the Post Office, I said, "When I grow up, I will work at the Post Office." Guess what? I did. Looking back at this, I understand the power of words at this stage. We speak and see things come forth.

I wanted these jobs to make money to help my parents and siblings. I worked at both places, the Post Office and Dupont. I was calling things forth. I believed that in my mind. My motives were pure and honest. I wanted to bring an increase to my family. That's what Jesus did for us as sons of God. I wanted to make life better for us and help my parents so their burdens would be light. They never asked me to do that, but my heart was to bring salvation to my family and freedom to my parents from hard work and long hours. I wanted my share in the family business.

We are heirs of God in Christ and joint-heirs with Jesus Christ. An heir gets a right to the father's inheritance following the father's death. Now, it is something that Jesus died on the cross, was resurrected from the dead, and received his inheritance. Romans 6:3–6 says that when Jesus died, we also died. When he was raised from the dead, we were raised from the dead. We reign with him in partnership. Romans 8:17 confirms that we are joint-heirs with Jesus Christ. So, whatever Jesus received as the firstborn from the dead, we share in it too. Being children of God, we are joint-heirs, leading us to sonship.

Galatians 4:6 says, "And because ye are sons, God hath sent forth the Spirit of his Son into your hearts, crying, Abba, Father."

Remember in a previous chapter, I wrote about my father's parents having their farm? Well, my grandparents died, my father died, and now that property belongs to my siblings and me. Right now, we share as joint-heirs with each other. Some family members do not realize the gift or inheritance their forefathers left them. Consider how Esau gave up his birthright to Jacob. He had no idea what he was forfeiting.

In Luke 15:32, even though the father was still alive, the son that most people identify as the prodigal son (though both sons actually were prodigals, each in their own way) asked his father for his inheritance. And the father separated a portion out to him. That son went out and wasted it all and came back home like a slave. He had nothing that identified him like royalty. And although he came home looking like a slave, his father never saw him that way. He had a big party for him. So, what we learn is that he had to leave his father's house to appreciate his father's house! I was like that. We were all like that.

Jesus came and died, ensuring we would share in the inheritance as God's sons. Thank you, Jesus. Now I am learning this while walking with God. I'm discovering what Jesus accomplished. Through Him, we have all the gifts that come with grace. Our inheritance is one of the most import-ant gifts of grace. It is unmerited and undeserved. We share the throne of Christ as joint-heirs. I am learning the benefits we have in Christ Jesus.

When I was born (purposed by God) into my natural family, that was no choice of my own. Not even the choice of my parents. God predestined those choices. Even so, with my heavenly family, I had no power to determine who they would be. I simply had to receive them. Jesus was the first choice from above. This had nothing to do with human works—it was a royal choice.

We are positioned in Christ Jesus. He is everything that humanity needs.

Chapter Eight

Freedom with Him

Wherefore come out from among them, and be
ye separate, saith the LORD, and touch not the
unclean thing; and I will receive you, and will be
a Father unto you, and ye shall be My sons and
daughters, saith the LORD Almighty.

(2 Corinthians 6:17–18)

I learned while walking with God and grew in spirit and
stature. I discovered what Jesus accomplished. I was daily
learning the benefits we have in Christ Jesus. But as you may
have, at first, I found my newly found freedom in Christ felt
like bondage, rejection, and loneliness. I had to adjust to spiritual freedom. I discovered three things about it. As I walked
with God, I understood greater truths about His separation,
endurance, and accountability.

SEPARATION

When it pleased God, He separated me from my mother's womb. I am not just talking about my natural mother. I was separated from religious traditions or man's way of thinking and living on the earth. We are to express Christ on the earth as His representatives, ambassadors, and spokespersons. This separation was to bring me into distinction, definition, and government. It did not place me above others. It placed me in the Lord's hand for a precise purpose and mission.

Separation has been a part of my walk most of my life. The greatest separation is to do Kingdom business. 2 Corinthians 6:17 says, " 'Wherefore come out from among them, and be ye separate,' saith the Lord, 'and touch not the unclean thing; and I will receive you.'" Also, Hebrews 7:26 says, "For such an high priest became us, who is holy, harmless, undefiled, separate from sinners, and made higher than the heavens."

ENDURANCE

Life processes and exposure to different changes brought forth a relationship with the One who called me by His grace. It's not a religious endeavor but my relationship with the great I Am through grace and faith in Jesus Christ. I discovered that my God was watching over me in all that I walked through. No matter how I saw myself or how much I accumulated in life, it was necessary for His plan and purpose. I had to learn who I am in Christ. I learned about the power (authority) that has been given to me. It is all found in Christ Jesus. James 1:3–4 says, "Knowing this, that the trying of your faith worketh patience. But let patience have her perfect work, that ye may be perfect and entire, wanting nothing." And 1 Peter 1:7 says, "That the trial of your faith, being much more precious than of gold that perisheth, though it be tried with fire, might be found unto praise and honour and glory at the appearing of Jesus Christ."

ACCOUNTABILITY

Accountability is one of life's most important lessons. I must give an account to the One who brought me through the difficult times of life by learning why I have been called, accepted, and justified. It was not just for me but for His purpose and plan. This knowledge has taught me that I must yield to God. A yielded life is a life lived by being accountable. It is reporting to the One who started the process. Life is a trust, a test, and a temporary assignment. To me, life is resting in the finished work of Jesus Christ.

Philippians 1:21 says, "For me to live is Christ, and to die is gain." Colossians 3:4 says, "When Christ, who is our life, shall appear, then shall ye also appear with him in glory." We must give an account to God as Romans 14:11–12 describes, "For it is written, As I live, saith the Lord, every knee shall bow to me, and every tongue shall confess to God." So, then every one of us shall give an account of himself to God.

Living the life of Christ prepares us for separation, endurance, and accountability.

Walking to God, walking with God, and walking as God's representative is about separation from less to something greater, or I should say... Someone greater.

Part Three

Walking as God

Chapter Nine

Learning Kingdom Life

But continue thou in the things which thou hast
learned and hast been assured of, knowing of whom
thou hast learned them.

(2 Timothy 3:14)

I had not heard about the Kingdom of God until much further in my walk. Learning about this relationship has taken me to another higher level of living. I had to learn the ways of my heavenly family just as I had learned the ways of my natural family. That happened through gaining knowledge of God and understanding of His Word.

Romans 12:2 says, "And be not conformed to this world: but be ye transformed by the renewing of your mind, that ye may prove what is that good, and acceptable, and perfect will of God." I saw in the Word that we must learn the ways of God's Kingdom, His ways of living, speaking, and walking.

So for me, everything had to change. My thoughts and the way I saw my life had to change.

Being an ambassador or representative of where I am from means that I must speak, operate, and walk as the Heavenly Father's representative. I am not to represent myself nor the place I live (earthly) but from where I came from, heavenly (the Father's bosom). Remember, we are seated together with Him in heavenly places! That's my position in Christ.

My citizenship (way of life) is from above. It is citizenship in the Kingdom of God. Philippians 3:20–21 says, "For our conversation is in heaven; from whence also we look for the Saviour, the Lord Jesus Christ: Who shall change our vile body, that it may be fashioned like unto his glorious body, according to the working whereby he is able even to subdue all things unto himself." This includes our duties, rights, and privileges as a citizen. We have great privileges. We have access by faith to the glory of God as a citizen of this great Kingdom. Romans 5:1–2 says, "Therefore being justified by faith, we have peace with God through our Lord Jesus Christ: By whom also we have access by faith into this grace wherein we stand, and rejoice in hope of the glory of God."

We are kings and priests of this new covenant. We rule and reign on God's behalf as His representatives on the earth. As God's ambassadors, we were chosen to speak as His oracle. 1 Peter 2:9–10 says, "But ye are a chosen generation, a royal priesthood, an holy nation, a peculiar people; that ye should shew forth the praises of him who hath called you out of darkness into his marvelous light; Which in time past were not a people, but are now the people of God: which had not obtained mercy, but now have obtained mercy." Revelation 5:10 says, "And hast made us unto our God kings and priests: and we shall reign on the earth."

Knowing that God wanted more for me, I discovered that I wanted more for myself. For a long time, all I heard about was dying and going to my sweet home in the by and by. That was all that many would preach. They would say, "Give your life to Jesus so you won't go to hell." But God's plan for us is bigger than that, it is to accept the finished work of Jesus and to be His ambassadors on the earth! Now that shined a new light on me. I represent the Father and do the Father's biddings—I care for the family business! This is not just me, but whoever calls on the name of the Lord and accepts Him as their Lord and Savior. Can you imagine any better way to live here on earth? Acts 17:28 tells us that, "in Him we live, move, and have our being… for we are also his offspring."

This is where I want to introduce the concept of walking as God, God's representative on the earth. Through Christ, we have authority, dominion, and power. As representatives or ambassadors, we speak what God says and do what he says to do. I'm not talking about entering God's essence. I am talking about manifesting the Heavenly Father's life in and on earth.

This is not about me or any other person. It's about Him and His plan. God's purpose was to have a corporate man made in His image and after His likeness. The Corporate Man (the Body of Christ) is to be His ambassador, ruling, reigning, and having dominion in the earth on His behalf. We are not here to take His place but we are to be an expression of Him in and on the earth.

I've learned about the divine nature that we have in Christ. In that equipping, we can do the family business (Kingdom business). 2 Peter 1:3–4 says, "According as His divine power hath given unto us all things that pertain unto life and godliness, through the knowledge of Him that hath called us to glory and virtue: Whereby are given unto us exceeding great and precious promises: that by these ye might be partakers of the divine nature, having escaped the corruption that is in the world through lust."

We will do greater things on the earth as Jesus promised, walking as God's representative. John 14:12 says, "Verily, verily, I say unto you, 'He that believeth on me, the works that I do shall he do also; and greater works than these shall he do; because I go unto my Father.'" Look at some of the greater things we would do:

We introduce our Heavenly Father to the earthly family, which gives them identity.

We declare the good news of the Father's Kingdom, our inheritance.

We are privileged to pray for the sick, seeing them healed and delivered by the teachings of God's Word.

His word is taught by the diversity of ministry gifts from Jesus. They are collectively called the fivefold Ministry (the Apostles, Prophets, Evangelists, Pastors, Teachers).

As these ministry gifts, we cause the family of God to be the expression of God. Holy Spirit's clear purpose for these gifts is written in Ephesians 4:12: "For the perfecting of the saints, for the work of the ministry, for the edifying of the body of Christ."

From a Governmental standpoint, this is our mission of walking as God's representatives on the earth. Learning this knowledge and information has caused me to want to represent my Heavenly Father well. There weren't many ministers teaching and preaching this truth in my early years. I wanted to learn the mystery of representation, and God provided the opportunity.

Let's go back to the divine nature concept. So, you mean this divine nature was living in me? As some would say, this was the straw that broke the camel's back. God had an appointed time for every stage in my life. This was also true of Christ. He raised Christ from the dead, and I was raised justified by him. He separated me from my family and friends and brought a divide among church people. But the God of the mountain was living in me. Thank you, Jesus! This truth is that because God's Spirit lives in me, it brings stability to my everyday living.

First Corinthians 3:16 says, "Know ye not that ye are the temple of God, and that the Spirit of God dwelleth in you?" So living or learning the kingdom life is that my God lives His life through me. Submitting to his will and desires is a great release from self-efforts. It took away working in the flesh, trying to keep Moses's 613 rules and laws. As I yield, I learn more and more about God's Kingdom life.

What a great life! I thank God for sending His Son, Jesus. Jesus is the model or pattern Son, showing us how to live this Kingdom life on earth. He did nothing except what He saw His Father do. He also said what He heard the Father say and believed all the Father said. Jesus' thoughts, words, and actions were those of the Father. That is our posture also.

Jesus was the reset for all humanity, and this is still God's plan. John 5:30 says, "I can of my own self do nothing: as I hear, I judge: and my judgment is just; because I seek not my own will, but the will of the Father which hath sent me." John 5:19 says, "Then answered Jesus and said unto them, Verily, verily, I say unto you, The Son can do nothing of himself, but what he seeth the Father do: for what things soever he doeth, these also doeth the Son likewise."

I'm not just waiting to enjoy life in my heavenly home. (And you do not have to wait either!) God wanted to dwell in me while I lived on earth. 2 Corinthians 6:16 says, "And what agreement hath the temple of God with idols? For ye are the temple of the living God; as God hath said I will dwell in them, and walk in them; and I will be their God, and they shall be my people." It is clear in Romans 6:8–10, "Now if we be dead with Christ, we believe that we shall also live with him: Knowing that Christ being raised from the dead dieth no more; death hath no more dominion over him. For in that he died, he died unto sin once: but in that he liveth, he liveth unto God."

It is good to know just how much God loves us! Before I ever cried out to God, Christ had already taken care of my inheritance, authority, and reigning position that I now have in Him. What a great revelation on being reconciled to God by the death, burial, and resurrection of Christ Jesus. I can now say (according to Galatians 2:20) that the life I live in the flesh, I live by the faith of the Son of God.

So, it's God's life living in me according to Jesus Christ and His obedience to the Father. Jesus' faith in the Father is my living power on this earth.

Some might have a problem when I say walking as God. Please know that I am not saying I am the Supreme Deity. But the life I live on earth is a God-type life, by His desire and design, one with His nature and ability resting fully in me. I am living as His representative and ambassador.

I can tell my family about this new life in Christ, of being a son, the offspring of God through Jesus Christ! It was preordained before the foundation of the world. It happened before a single law was given or the first man formed.

Still not convinced that you can walk as God in this way? Check out the men and women in Hebrews 11. Note the elders that obtained a good report. Abel, Enoch, Noah, Abraham, Sarah, and the rest. They all died in faith, despite not receiving the promises in this earthly expression of life. The Bible says they 'saw them afar off,' were persuaded of them, embraced them, and confessed of a better country and city prepared for them by God.

We can find that same Truth witnessed in other scriptures, including Revelation 21:2, in which John writes, "And I John saw the holy city, new Jerusalem, coming down from God out of heaven, prepared as a bride adorned for her husband." So living this Kingdom life is the highest level of living. In Christ, we enter in to our heavenly home, country, and city, which is God's Kingdom (the New Jerusalem).

The elders in faith discovered that it is impossible to please God without faith. We discover the same as we are living as His representative and ambassador. Daily I am led and directed by His inner voice that says, "This is the way; walk in it."

We accept these things by faith and then walk as God—His anointed Shaliah, His ordained and appointed representatives.

Chapter Ten
Inheritance, Authority, Reigning

And hast made us unto God kings and priests: and
we shall reign on the earth.

(Revelation 5:10)

Now, years into my life, I am in this fellowship and relationship with God. I've learned much but I am still learning
about my inheritance. I am in God's Will as a son. I also
have many benefits, not just salvation from sin; I have healing, deliverance, and the wholeness of life. That knowledge
is good—this is a beginning—but it does not compare to
sharing in the family business! Other benefits are a sense of
identity, security, purpose, acceptance, continual forgiveness,
provision, and… being chosen!

After many years, I am now at a place in God where I
can be trusted to handle kingdom business as His ambassador or representative on the earth. We are like ambassadors

sent to another country to represent and stand on behalf of their country. Each country calls its ambassador and charges that person to represent and speak as the country's authority. They have the authority to operate in another country as the one who sent them. The representative does not operate on his thoughts or ideas in another country but stands in the sender's place.

Let's understand what it means to be a representative or ambassador. They are credentialed diplomats serving as a foreign country's official representatives or promoters. While taking care of the sender's business, there are benefits that one receives. The country from which one is from takes care of the representative completely. For example, I am one of God's ambassadors; we are here on a mission to declare kingdom affairs. So, Matthew 6:25 instructs us, "Therefore I say unto you, 'Take no thought for your life, what ye shall eat, or what ye shall drink; nor yet for your body, what ye shall put on. Is not the life more than meat, and the body than raiment?'" The country you represent is responsible for ensuring you are protected, cared for, and have what you need to survive while sent to a foreign land.

Kingdom ambassadors learn in Matthew 6:33 to "seek first the kingdom of God and his righteousness, and all these things will be added unto" them. You must know and understand your country if you are to represent that country well. You must study "all the ins and outs" to give the best representation possible. You are standing in your position for an entire country. You are in constant contact with your country's higher authorities and official leaders. You must study to make sure a thorough representation is done well.

How do we do this as a Kingdom representative? Know your Sender's heart, will, and policies entirely, which in God's Kingdom is the Word of God. Speak as one having authority and power to operate the affairs of whom you represent. (The officials will not send one ignorant of its affairs but ones who are well abreast of what that country can offer.) These are those who can articulate well and have influence. Remember that the ambassador is in that position as his leader, not for himself but for a higher power. I must remember I am subject to a higher power and must rule at the higher power's command. I am not my own.

An ambassador in God's Kingdom is a voice for the Kingdom of God, one who is walking to God (getting to know Him), walking with God (being a co-laborer and partaker of the inheritance), and walking as God (ruling, reigning, and representing God in His affairs).

Chapter Eleven

Freedom in Him, In Christ

For God so loved the world…

(John 3:16)

What I experienced in my early life prepared me for Kingdom Living. I was acquainted with disappointments, rejections, limitations, speaking before an audience, and dealing with fears. The list goes on. God's plan is never fruitless but fruitful. He chose my path, and now I am grateful. All that I learned has been life-changing. I thank God for every door He opened and every door He closed.

The cover and illustrations in this book were chosen deliberately, for I am (and you are) like a butterfly. I am free in Christ Jesus. Jesus set me free. He made me free before I knew I was free. I walked into my freedom. Now I know it is not conditioned on my love for him, but rather, during the process, I discovered that in every stage of development,

I am securely anchored by His Love for me—unconditional, unmerited, and unearned Love.

People would say, "You are so free!" I would say, "Jesus made me free." I couldn't explain what that meant to me because people were always in a hurry. But I can explain it to you here. Gaining the knowledge of Kingdom life is what made me free. This is only found in the death, burial, and resurrection of Jesus Christ. In getting to know Him, I encountered my newly created resurrected life!

I will say it again. I was free before I knew I was free. I had not only freedom but I was made righteous. I was made free and righteous not of works of my own but because of the finished work of Jesus Christ in that he pleased the Father. Just like I had no choice in my earthly parents and family, I had no choice in His gift of my righteousness and freedom. My part was only to agree with Him by saying, "Amen, I believe it, and receive it."

Everything was planned and set up before I came into the world, including my position in Christ and God's Kingdom Plan. Agree with God and Live! That's my motto.

Knowing this freedom brought an end to the fears that plagued me. In Jesus, I am whole, completely accepted, and approved. I am a part of His beloved. It is such a deep joy to know that! I realize that many today, perhaps you, need to hear that as well.

Freedom comes in agreeing with God, and that freedom will change how people see themselves, just like it did for me.

I can look in the mirror and say, "I am free, loved, and His son (offspring)." Saying I am free brings so much liberty. I'm not wondering if men accept me or how they see me. They don't carry so much weight with me now. I say to myself, "I am beautifully and wonderfully made in Christ." I know that I have peace with God, whether men approve or not. I know that I am accepted by the Beloved. Like the stages of the butterfly depicted in the chapters of this book of testimony, every stage of my life brought me to my purpose and destiny.

If you can just get a vision of what God sees in you, you might change how you see yourself. Truth will make you free. Man can agree with you or not, but you have to say to yourself, "I am what God says I am, and I can do what God says I can do."

It starts with a vision, confession, and transformation. The power of words that you say to yourself can change everything. Agreeing with what God says can cause two to walk together because they agree. (Amos 3:3.)

I say again to you (like I say to myself), "Agree with God and live!"

Chapter Twelve

Who I Am As Son

Herein is our love made perfect, that we may have
boldness in the day of judgment: because as He is,
so are we in this world.

(1 John 4:17)

I thank God for my parents and family. They instilled a
sense of greatness in me. Greatness means knowing who I am
as God's son (offspring). My earthly parents provided values
on how to handle the family business. That is also the heart
of God, especially for His sons who must walk as their Father
on the earth. We reign in our position in Him. We are His
royalty, the King's offspring of full age to handle the family business. When we speak what God says, we know that
Word will be fulfilled and come to pass. We speak boldly—
not intimidated or indecisively but with confidence. I know
God! We are one. The life that I live is Christ. The trumpet

(mouthpiece) sounds—I am declaring His Word (messages), walking as God, being His ambassador and representative, speaking, teaching, and demonstrating in Him, for Him, as Him.

When I was first commissioned to start a Kingdom work, the Lord said, "Teach my people as I would." I said, "I can't do that; I don't know how." He said, "Love them as I would love them." I said, "I cannot love them like you." He said, "I will do it through you." So, I had to submit to the mighty God. "Lord, I am your vessel." In myself, I could not do that. He equipped and is still equipping me to do just that as I continue submitting to His will.

Paul says, "For me to live is Christ" (Philippians 1:21). To me, that statement meant living here on earth is Christ. The life I live is by the faith of the Son of God. As He lives, so do I! Being one with His Word is being one with God. It is to be reconciled with the Father and reconciled with Jesus Christ. He went to the cross as the sacrificial offering (Lamb). When he died, I died. When he was buried, I was buried. I also rose in victory by faith when he rose from the grave!

When I asked Jesus to come into my life as my Lord and Savior, I was reconciled to the Father. If Jesus is one with the Father, I am one with the Father. We are the sons of God. We are equal in God—Jesus is not ashamed to call us brothers. (Take time to read Hebrews 2:11–12.) We are His body; we must put on His mind and think like Jesus. Philippians 2:5–6 says, "Let this mind be in you, which was also in

Christ Jesus: Who, being in the form of God, thought it not robbery to be equal with God." And Ephesians 5:1–2 says, "Imitate God as dear children." God has both asked us to do so and equipped us to do so!

In 2008, my only son had a heart attack that brought him closer to God. The event was a catalyst for his developing a strong relationship with God. He went on to walk with God. He watched us closely and mimicked us in our actions and speech. He delivered his first message, "You Must Be Born Again." From that moment forward, he honored us by calling us apostles. It was such a significant change in his life.

He had another heart attack in 2012, but this one was the big one. He stayed in the hospital for two and a half months. I got to know this newly created son of God, which was my son. On February 15, he had a severe attack that put him in a coma. I sat beside his bed, praying continually.

I remembered an incident in 2 Kings 4:32–37. Elisha laid on top of the Shunammite woman's son, who had died, and he was raised to life by Elisha laying on top of him and breathing new life into him. Well, I thought I would do as Elisha did! But then, my human mind kicked in and said, "What would the doctors and nurses say if they came in and saw me doing that?" I thought, "I would be called crazy, laughed at, and ridiculed!" So, I said to myself, "I can't do that." I was cheated out of that miracle. My son died, and we celebrated his life. I prayed that God would give me another chance to see a miracle. I desired to see the glory of God manifested on this earth.

In 2015 another opportunity, the doctor diagnosed my dad with lung cancer. The doctor said it would grow rapidly and overtake his entire lungs. I had said, "God give me another opportunity to see your glory." So, some of my family members joined together and prayed that the growth would stop, and it did. It never grew any further. That was what we all asked! God answered that prayer for us based on what we prayed.

My faith grew to speak His Word and see something we had never seen before. So, my faith leaped; we rejoiced that the growth of cancer had stopped. My faith was growing to speak His Word, and things were happening. This level of faith was above that level of faith with my son. Yes, my dad transitioned, but there was a change in me to believe in God for greater things. From my son's transition to my dad's transition, I recognized that my level of faith had enlarged. Today, I believe that we would have received more if we had asked for more.

There is an interesting story that occurs in 2 Kings 13:14–19. Just before Elisha died, Jehoash, king of Israel, came before him and received instructions about defeating the Syrian king. Elisha commanded the king to take an arrow and smite the ground. He smote the ground three times and stopped. The prophet became wroth. He said, "If you had smitten the ground five or six times, you would have had that many victories over Syria." Jehoash cut himself short because of the limitation in his mind.

In 2019, I was confronted with another opportunity to see the glory of God manifest. My husband, Fred, was experiencing health difficulties. The doctors diagnosed him with Stage 4 cancer. When we both heard that, for a moment, it hit me, "CANCER! Oh my goodness, not the big C." Immediately, my emotions became overwhelmed with that news. It was like I was dreaming. I asked my husband, "Honey, can I cry?" (Can you imagine asking for permission to cry?) I had one good cry and then rose to my newly created self in Christ.

Remember above when I said, "I believe that we would have received more if we had asked for more?" So, this is what I asked, "Lord, is this Fred's time to leave?" I also said, "I don't want to serve in the ministry alone." The Lord comforted me. He said, "This is not a sickness unto death but will only last six months." I began to speak. God said our faith is being tested. God took us to another level of faith. We stood on His Word like never before. We took authority over our minds and bodies, declaring how much God loved us.

That cancer only lasted six months. My husband went through chemo and everything that the doctor prescribed. He lost so much weight. He was skin and bones. When God said this would only last six months, our faith turned to firmly standing and looking at Him.

Now, I will tell you... something was happening to our faith! We surrounded ourselves with nothing but the Word of God and like-minded people to keep watering and feeding our faith. That trial unlocked another level of growth and trust in our Heavenly Father.

In all these testimonies, in my life's stories of walking to God, the accounts of my walking with God, and the testimonies of our walking as God on the earth, my hope is that you are hearing Holy Spirit speaking to your heart. I pray He is reminding you of His faithfulness in your own life and showing (revealing) in your life's memories the times He was leading, guiding, and providing for you in your own walk.

God wants us to know him more intimately and excellently; He wants us to speak as His representative. This takes nothing from God of who He is. Heaven and earth must be One. We speak what heaven has released and must bind what heaven has declared unlawful.

We must release what heaven has permitted to come to the earth. Heaven and earth must be one. We must walk, talk, and act as God's representative—His fully authorized Shaliah—to fully represent Him and carry on the Kingdom Business—God's Family Business.

God is Spirit, but we express Him on the earth. We are His offspring on earth. Walking to God joins you to what He always had planned in you, for you, and through you. Walking with God develops you to know and love Him, the One who keeps you in your innermost parts. Walking as God is the result of His revelation blossoming in you. Walking as God walks is not arrogance. It is not presumptuousness. It is our assignment as sons of God. We are talking about our position in Christ Jesus—one of ruling and reigning on Earth on His behalf.

Life is a trust, a test, and a temporary assignment: **We are to be the visibility of the invisible God.**

As He is, so are we on the earth.

(1 John 4:17)

Meet the Author

In this book, which is part memoir and part exhortation, the author, Apostle Marcia E. Rhoe, invites you into an intimate look at her own life's transformation. Filled with testimonies of God's wondrous love, this book will speak to you of real lives that have proven Him faithful.

Apostle Rhoe weaves a beautiful tapestry of transforming truth that shows how He who began a good work in us is well able to perform it. And what is our role? We must trust the process… The Metamorphosis of Purpose!

Just like the butterfly's life stages, from egg to caterpillar, to chrysalis to butterfly, God has taken her life through His amazing transforming miracle plan. Along the journey, she has learned and experienced first-hand that His plan is to bring us to **His expected end**. You will often hear her say, *"Life is a trust, a test, and a temporary assignment."*

Apostle Marcia E. Rhoe, a native of Kinston, N.C., has been pastoring Destiny Ministries since 1998, serving in team ministry, as One, with her husband, Apostle Frederick Rhoe.

In all endeavors, her heart is to invest God's love into a corporate family, teaching them how to administrate the

family business, *the Kingdom of God*. Her passion is to build and empower God's people, develop Kingdom ambassadors, and present our King in every facet of life.

To invite Apostle Marcia Rhoe to speak
or to purchase additional copies,
please visit :

drmarciarhoe.org   or
destinyministriesinc.org

You may contact the author directly:

Apostle Marcia Rhoe
PO BOX 215
Kinston NC 28502

www.ingramcontent.com/pod-product-compliance
Lightning Source LLC
Chambersburg PA
CBHW020424130626
46549CB00006B/2718